THE
CHEROKEES
PAST AND PRESENT
An Authentic Guide To The Cherokee People

By J. Ed. Sharpe
Illustrations by Shirley Simmons

Copyright© 1970
Cherokee Publications

ɔx 430

Cherokee, N. C.

1

INTRODUCTION

So exciting and colorful is the past and present of th Cherokee Indian People that it would seem appropriate for a persons to have the opportunity to study them in accuracy an authenticity.

Present knowledge is, on the contrary, neither authentic n accurate as understood by most people. The very means of mas media that should make our understanding more complete ha rather distorted and discolored the history, culture, and prese circumstances of the American Indian, including the Cheroke

It is the intention of this booklet to present both an accura and easily readable account of one of the most colorful ar interesting empires of this continent in the pre-white man er

All cannot be told on these brief pages, but enough perhap to correct common fallacies and offer the reader a challengir introduction to his study of the Cherokee people.

The author is greatly indebted to the Cherokee Historic Association for their helpful assistance and cooperation in th preparation of this book, and for the use of their excellent pictur found throughout the following pages.

Deep appreciation and gratitude is expressed also to M Thomas B. Underwood, whose technical advice, careful guidanc and constant encouragement has helped to make this book reality.

CONTENTS

CHEROKEE

◆◆◆◆◆◆◆◆◆◆◆◆◆◆◆◆◆◆

Nearly ten thousand yea
ago, when the giant glaciers an
bitter cold of the last Ice Ag
were declining, the forefathe
of the Cherokees made the
way from Asia to this continer
Over a narrow strip of lan
now covered by the Bering Stra
they wandered into Nor
America as nomadic tribes, fo
lowing herds of wild prehistor
animals and seeking to kee
themselves alive.

Spreading southward like a gigantic fan of humanity, the
wandering tribes continued to come, populating most of Nor
and South America. Differing in appearance, languag
and customs, they came eventually to call certain areas of th
new continent their home.

It is believed that the Cherokees and Iroquois are broth
tribes, having come from the same source. They were known f
their superior height and robust stature. Claiming for their huntin
grounds what is now parts of eight states, the Cherokees becam
the mightiest Indian Empire of all the Southeastern Tribes. Grad
ally their towns grew up near the mouths of small streams whe
clear water was plentiful.

When the first white man, Hernando De Soto, came in
Cherokee country in the sixteenth century there were abo
25,000 Cherokees. This Spanish adventurer, coming into t
Cherokee mountain territory in search of gold, began the lo
and painful march of the white man into the Cherokees' worl

The influx of settlers pushed hard against the Cherokees, a
in a series of treaties from 1684 to 1835, consistently broke
the Cherokee country shrank from an empire of enormous pr
portions to a small boundary in Western North Carolina.

The saddest winter in Cherokee history was that of 1838-3
when the Indian people were taken from their homes, herde
like cattle, and moved to Oklahoma through the bitter wint
weather. Over 4,000 Cherokees died due to this action of t
government. So sad and tragic was the journey that it is calle
even today, the "Trail of Tears."

A brief outline of dates and significant events are listed c
the opposite page for a birds-eye view of the Cherokee histor

RIGIN AND HISTORY

-8000 B.C. ... Nomadic tribes wandered into this continent from Asia.

40 A.D. .... First white man, DeSoto of Spain, entered Cherokee country.

84 .... First treaty made with the Cherokees.

38 .... Small Pox killed nearly half of the Cherokee population.

43 .... First missionary came to the Cherokees—Christian Priber.

73 .... Three treaties took most of the Cherokee lands.

76 .... Cherokee driven into the Smokies; their homes, crops, live-stock, and towns destroyed by settlers.

12 .... Cherokees fought against the Creek Indians.

14 .... Cherokees assisted Andrew Jackson in defeating the Creeks at Horseshoe Bend.

21 .... Sequoyah's alphabet approved by the Cherokee chiefs.

27 .... Led by Chief John Ross the Cherokees adopted a national constitution.

28 .... First edition of the **Cherokee Phoenix** printed in both Chero-kee and English.

35 .... Treaty for Removal signed by a handful of Cherokees.

38-39 .... The "Trail of Tears" to Oklahoma caused the death of four thousand Cherokees.

43-61 .... Will Thomas purchased land for the Cherokees remaining in North Carolina and held the deeds for them.

76 .... Qualla Boundary formed and Cherokee lands secured.

39 .... Rights of Cherokees established by North Carolina Legisla-ture. Charter granted and The Eastern Band of Cherokees formed.

24 .... By petition of the tribal council the Federal Government took the lands of the Cherokees into trust.

CHEROKEE LANGUAGE

Cherokee is a unique language of rising and falling tones spoken with hardly a movement of the lips. Though gutteral and at places very difficult, it has a beauty all its own.

The Cherokee and Iroquoian languages evolved from the same mother tongue. The later Cherokee language developed into three distinct dialects:

Elati ....Eastern Dialect ....Now extinct
Kituhwa ....Middle Dialect ....Used in Western N.C.
Atali ....Western Dialect ....Used in Oklahoma

The many tribes of Indian people had only spoken languages and they used pictures rather than letters and words to record their tribal history.

Among the Cherokees, however, a man by the name of Sequoyah had a dream of making a "talking leaf" like that of the white man. Sequoyah whose English name was George Guess, was an illiterate, but solely out of his personal genius and determination he created a Cherokee alphabet or Syllabary and endowed his entire tribe with a written language.

After twelve years of dogged persistence and hard work, Sequoyah produced a syllabary of eighty five symbols, each representing a sound in the Cherokee spoken language. His alphabet was approved by the Cherokee chiefs in 1821, and in very short time the entire tribe was reading and writing in the new language. The New Testament was translated and a newspaper begun.

Today the Cherokee language has given away to the more practical and necessary use of English which the children use at school. Some of the older people still prefer to speak in their native tongue, however, and efforts are being made to keep it alive.

Cherokee Syllabary

ᏣᎳᎩ ᏗᎪᏪᎶᏗ

a	e	i	o	u	v
Ꭰ *a*	Ꭱ *e*	Ꭲ *i*	Ꮐ *o*	Ꭴ *u*	Ꭵ *i*
Ꭶ *ga* Ꭷ *ka*	Ꭸ *ge*	Ꭹ *gi*	Ꭺ *go*	Ꭻ *gu*	Ꭼ *gv*
Ꭽ *ha*	Ꭾ *he*	Ꭿ *hi*	Ꮀ *ho*	Ꮁ *hu*	Ꮂ *hv*
Ꮃ *la*	Ꮄ *le*	Ꮅ *li*	Ꮆ *lo*	Ꮇ *lu*	Ꮈ *lv*
Ꮉ *ma*	Ꮊ *me*	Ꮋ *mi*	Ꮌ *mo*	Ꮍ *mu*	
Ꮎ *na* Ꮏ *hna* Ꮐ *nah*	Ꮑ *ne*	Ꮒ *ni*	Ꮓ *no*	Ꮔ *nu*	Ꮕ *nv*
Ꮖ *qwa*	Ꮗ *qwe*	Ꮘ *qwi*	Ꮙ *qwo*	Ꮚ *qwu*	Ꮛ *qwv*
Ꮜ *sa* Ꮝ *s*	Ꮞ *se*	Ꮟ *si*	Ꮠ *so*	Ꮡ *su*	Ꮢ *sv*
Ꮣ *da* Ꮤ *ta*	Ꮥ *de* Ꮦ *te*	Ꮧ *di* Ꮨ *ti*	Ꮩ *do*	Ꮪ *du*	Ꮫ *dv*
Ꮬ *dla* Ꮭ *tla*	Ꮮ *tle*	Ꮯ *tli*	Ꮰ *tlo*	Ꮱ *tlu*	Ꮲ *tlv*
Ꮳ *tsa*	Ꮴ *tse*	Ꮵ *tsi*	Ꮶ *tso*	Ꮷ *tsu*	Ꮸ *tsv*
Ꮹ *wa*	Ꮺ *we*	Ꮻ *wi*	Ꮼ *wo*	Ꮽ *wu*	Ꮾ *wv*
Ꮿ *ya*	Ᏸ *ye*	Ᏹ *yi*	Ᏺ *yo*	Ᏻ *yu*	Ᏼ *yv*

ᏍᏛ ᎤᏙᏍᏂ ᏴᎣᏂ ᏗᏨᎵᏓᏒ
ᎠᎯ ᎭᎠᏉᎤᏣ ᎠᎤᏬᎠᏂ
ᎠᏳᏍᏱᏓᏴ. ᎥᎤᏴ ᏎᏬᏢᏁ
ᏓᏫᎳᎢ ᎠᏍ ᏕᎦᏁ
ᏎᎤ ᏗᎣᏃᏴᎩ

PSALM 121:1-2

I WILL LIFT UP MINE EYES UNTO THE HILLS, FROM WHENCE COMETH MY HELP. MY HELP COMETH FROM THE LORD, WHICH MADE HEAVEN AND EARTH.

PSALM 121:1-2

7

CHEROKEE

From very early times much of the Cherokee's food came from the wild plants found in abundance in their woodland environment. Preparation of such foods developed into an art among the Indian women. Among the wild plant foods listed below are some that are still used today by the mountain people.

WILD PLANT FOODS

Persimmons	Strawberries	Chestnuts
Plums	Honey Locusts	Hickory Nuts
Grapes	Wild Potatoes	Walnuts
Blackberries	Smilax Roots	Wild Greens
Mulberries	Mushrooms	Other roots and herbs
Huckleberries		

The beginning of gardening, or planned crop raising, came when Indian people discovered plants growing from refuse that they had discarded. Gradually the art of planting, tending, and harvesting crops developed.

Basic among the food they raised was corn, called by the Cherokee, Selu. So important was it to their lives that many religious ceremonies, including the Green and Ripe Corn Feasts, were held in its honor.

GARDEN CROPS

Corn	Sunflowers (for oil and meal)
Beans	Tobacco (for ceremonial use)
Pumpkins	Gourds (for utensils)
Squashes	

"Sugar" needs were provided for by the use of maple sap, honey, and honey-locust pods. Salt was derived from salt licks in Kentucky and from salt springs in Tennessee.

FOODS

The Cherokee hunter was very skilled in the killing of wild game. Using bows and arrows, masks, decoys, blowguns, spears, and traps, he claimed the animals and adapted every part of them to his use. Meat, hides, bones, claws, and antlers all found their useful place in the Cherokee camp.

WILD GAME FOODS

Deer	Rabbit	Also:	Crayfish
Bear	Squirrel		Frogs
Wild Turkey	Birds		Bird's Eggs
Bison	Elk		Yellow-jacket grubs
Groundhog	Wolf (for hides)		Cicadas

Trout, catfish, redhorse, and a variety of other fish were abundant in the mountain streams and rivers around the Cherokee settlements. The men and boys devised means for catching them, giving them a very welcome place among the Cherokee foods.

FISHING DEVICES

Hooks.......fashioned from bones.

Thread .....spun from animal hair and bark fibers.

Weirs ....stone walls where fish were driven through opening and caught.

Poison......fish were stunned by poison from chestnuts, walnut roots, bark, and other materials, and caught by hand.

Hands ......fish were caught by hand while wading in shallow water.

CHEROKEE

Contrary to popular thought, th
Cherokees did not live in Teepees or Wig
wams. Such dwellings were characteristic of th
western Plains Indians who needed to keep thei
homes portable as they often moved about.

The Cherokee were a more settled people with establishe
villages along the mountain rivers. Their homes were made b
placing large posts for uprights about two or three feet apar
Smaller posts were set between the large ones. Using limbe
twigs or split canes they interwove them between the posts, makin
basket-like walls.

Grass, mixed in smooth clay, was plastered over the walls. Th
roof was made in almost the same way, but it was covered wit
bark or thatch.

In the center of the floor inside the house a basin was scoope
out for a fireplace, and a circular stone placed beside it to b
used in making bread. A hole in the roof about three inches i
diameter allowed the smoke to escape.

Beds were constructed at one end of the house using sho
posts for legs and woven white oak or ash splints for the fram
Hemlock boughs, broomsage, and similar soft materials wer
placed under woven mats for bedding, and buffalo, beaver, an
other skins provided warm coverings.

At the other end of the house the family stored their po
sessions. An animal skin or a mat covered the small doorwa

DWELLINGS

Some of the people had storehouses for dried food. These were made after the pattern of the dwellings except much smaller and were erected on posts several feet from the ground.

Each family had a hothouse in which they slept during cold weather. It was constructed of an earth covered framework over an excavation in the ground. Benches around the edges served as beds, and a fire burned in the center all day to heat the house for sleeping during the night. The hot house was used for certain ceremonial purposes also, and it was around the hothouse fire that the "myth-keepers" recited the sacred legends of their past.

The Cherokees, in colonial times, copied the log houses of the settlers and became very expertise in the making of them from native timber.

CHEROKEE

In ancient times the Cherokees adapted the skins of wild animals for clothing, but long before the white man put his foot on the American continent the Cherokees had learned to spin various types of animal hair and bark fibers into thread for weaving. Although the records of pre white man clothing are limited, we do have some indication of what the Cherokee people were wearing before the first explorer came into their country.

MEN
Deerskin shirts in summer.
Panther, Bear, Beaver, Otter, and Buckskin in winter (fur turned in).
High Deerskin boots.
Deerskin breech clouts.
Moccasins.
Short feather cloaks.
Mantles, belted at the waist.
Hair shaved or plucked out except for a small patch on top

WOMEN
Wrap-around skirt of deerskin.
Buffalo calfskin in winter (hair turned in).
Drape, over left shoulder covering the upper body.
Trim of feathers and other ornaments.
Skirts of turkey feathers held together by strips of bark.
Primary colors were red and yellow.
Hair was worn long.

YOUNG MEN AND WOMEN
Often wore a six foot square of cloth with a wide border, wrapping it around them like a Roman toga.

WARRIORS
Bands of otter skin on head, arm, and legs.
Red feathers stuck under the headband.
Wore clothing as indicated above for men.
Carried weapons as described on pages 22 and 23.

CLOTHING

THE CHEROKEE CHIEF

The Cherokee Chief was always elaborately and distinctively dressed. The peace or civil chief was installed in yellow, but he customarily wore white. The war chief wore red and kept a raven's skin around his neck. Other items of the Chiefs' dress included:

Leather shirt coming down to the hips.
Leather breech clout fastened at the sides.
Leather belt that reached twice around his waist and had long tassels.
Leather leggins.
Garters.
Moccasins with small bells attached.
Long cloak fastened at both shoulders.
Cap of otter skin with a leather band. Covered with white crane feathers.
Sleeves of Raccoon skins.
Strings of deer hoofs around the ankles.
Leather tobacco pouch.
Carried a wand of crane or swan wings.

ORNAMENTS

Beads	Glass
Bracelets	Shell
Bone Pendants	Stone Discs
Bone	Ear bobs
Silver	Feathers
Gold	Animal Hair
Rings	

The Cherokee people had become ingenious in the making of clothing from the materials available to them in their natural environment. They were quick, however, to adapt the clothing of European explorers and settlers to their use, but even today one can easily notice a generous use of leather shirts and jackets among them.

CHEROKEE

Over many centuries the Cherokee people developed an incredible ability to work with their hands. Using native materials to construct useful articles they became artists of distinctive designs and expert craftsmen in the making of jewelry, pottery, baskets, woodwork, and weapons.

JEWELRY

The Cherokee, like most of the Indian peoples, made much use of jewelry and ornaments in their hair, on their clothing, and about their necks, wrists, and ankles. In ancient times they used shells, seeds, bone, teeth, stones, and feathers to make such ornaments.

Glass beads were introduced to the Cherokees by the very first explorers, however, and they quickly became expert in devising and executing beautiful and colorful patterns for belts headbands, and other jewelry.

Beadwork, made in the same artistic and creative way by the Cherokee people, is still available today in areas where the Cherokee live.

POTTERY

Pipes, bowls, jars, pots, and similar items for practical and ceremonial use were made from the native clay. The clay was dug, dried by the fire, and pulverized into a powder. The powder was then mixed with water to a consistency suitable for working

The Cherokees never used a potter's wheel, but fashioned their pottery with their fingers, sometimes coiling strips of clay upward from the base to the rim and then blending it together.

A carved wooden paddle was used to imprint designs, and a smooth stone employed to polish the surface, making it waterproof.

The pots were fired outside using bark and native woods. The kind of wood used in the fire determined the color the pot would be. Bran or broken corncobs were thrown into the red-hot pots to smoke them and make them waterproof inside.

14

BASKETRY

The Cherokees are famous among Indian peoples for their skillful weaving of baskets, and their development of intricate and beautiful patterns for them. The process of gathering materials for weaving and dying, preparing the materials, and actually weaving baskets of distinctive designs is a difficult and time-consuming one.

Materials used by the basketweavers include:

Honeysuckle vines
White Oak splints
Ash splints
Rivercane
Bark
Wild Hemp

Dyes from:
Blood root
Yellow root
Oak and Maple Bark
Poison Ivy root
Wild Celandine Poppy roots
Sassafras roots
Walnut bark
Butterfly roots

CARVING

Native wood and stone offered the Cherokee raw material for the fashioning of masks, pendants, pipes, canoes, weapons and tools. They became quite proficient in the making of such articles. Intricate designs were developed as many found on their pipestems, pottery, paddles, and pendants.

Wood and stone carvers among the Cherokee today often get national recognition for their work. Animal and figurine sculpture is still being made and sold in the Cherokee area.

Many craftsmen can be seen at their work at the Oconaluftee Living Indian Village in Cherokee, North Carolina.

KENTUCKY

TENNESSEE

PRESE
CHER

SOUTH

ALABAMA

GEORGIA

The Chero

ORIGINAL CHEROKEE
CHEROKEE BOUNDARY
CHEROKEE BOUNDARY
PRESENT CHEROKEE

WEST
VIRGINIA

VIRGINIA

NORTH CAROLINA

SER ATION

NA

e Country

SE OF REVOLUTION
AL CESSION
ATION (QUALLA BOUNDARY)

CHEROKEE GOVERNMENT

Even though the Cherokee empire was vast, it had a national government that was effective and efficient. It was divided into a peace or civil organization and a war organization. Each main town maintained its own system of government on the local level patterned after the national one.

The chief was head of the nation in both a civil and a religious capacity. He had two primary men who ruled with him, his Right Hand Man and a Speaker, both of whom held seats beside him in the Council House. The Right Hand Man, along with six other men, formed a group of seven counselors to the chief.

Thus, the main government was composed of nine people. There were, however, seven honored women who shared in the government. Their duties included deciding whether a war captive would be killed or adopted into the tribe.

"Seven" was a very significant and sacred number to the Cherokee people. In addition to the seven counselors and seven women there were seven Cherokee clans, seven mother towns to serve as clan headquarters, and a seven-sided council house with a section of seats for representatives from each clan. The council house held approximately five hundred people and was off-limits to all but designated officials.

Clan membership was inherited from one's mother and retained for life. Each person had a close relationship with four of the seven clans: the mother's clan (of which he was a member), the father's clan, the paternal grandfather's clan, and the maternal grandfather's clan. A person was expected to marry into one of the latter two of these four clans. Marriages took place in the council house with a priest officiating.

In any single town all of the clans were represented, and all members of any one clan considered themselves to be brothers and sisters. Clan membership was indicated by the color of feathers one wore.

The civil-peace government conducted the religious ceremonies of the tribe and acted in both a judicial and legislative capacity, holding court and making laws. Murder and inter-clan marriage were both punishable by death.

Most criminal acts, however, were avenged by members of the wronged family and were seldom left up to the government.

In times of war a war chief, Kalanu, and his organization replaced the civil-peace organization. The war organization always wore red. The peace chief, though installed in yellow, customarily wore white.

THE SEVEN CLANS

WILD POTATO .. A NI GA TO GE WI
BIRD .... A NI TSI S KWA
LONG HAIR .... A NI GI LO HI
BLUE .... A NI SA HO NI
PAINT .... A NI WO DI
DEER .... A NI KA WI
WOLF .... A NI WA YAH

The Cherokee people called themselves **Ani Yunwiya** which means "Principal People." They formed the largest single tribe in the South. The name Cherokee, meaning "People who speak another language" was given them by other Indian tribes. They adopted the name themselves as Tsalagi.

Today the chief is elected by the people; all townships, some retaining clan names, are represented on the tribal council.

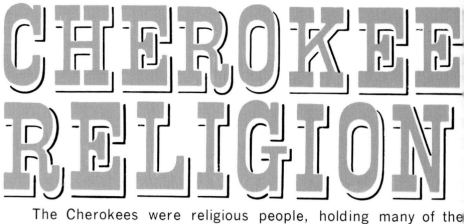

CHEROKEE RELIGION

The Cherokees were religious people, holding many of the things in their natural world to be sacred. Stories kept alive from generation to generation told of spiritual beings who created the earth, sun, moon, and stars. The one supreme being was named YOWA, a name so sacred that only certain priests were allowed to say it aloud. YOWA was a unity of three beings referred to as "The Elder Fires Above" (CHO TA AUH NE LE EH).

When the creator god, YOWA, had given form to the earth he left the sun and the moon to govern the world. They in turn appointed fire to take care of mankind using smoke as its messenger.

A belief in spirits and in the afterlife was strong and a person's spirit was thought to retrace his places of residence after he had died.

A Priest was singled out from childhood for very special religious training. He was taught the use of herbs and of the sacred quartz crystals used in religious practice. The most sacred objects were kept in the council house, including the "ark," probably containing a large quartz crystal.

Very little of the ancient ceremony or religion exists today. As a whole the Cherokee people have embraced the Christian religion and have a significant number of churches of various denominations on the Reservation.

The belief in the Great Spirit made the movement toward Christianity an easy one.

20

THINGS SACRED TO THE CHEROKEES

Eagle
Eagle Feathers
Rattlesnake
Fire
Smoke
Sun
Moon
Corn
"Seven"
Quartz Crystals
The Ark

EAGLE DANCER

The Eagle wand was a peace symbol. It was made of Eagle feathers and sourwood, both considered sacred materials. Only a professional Eagle-Killer could kill the Eagle, and then only with proper ceremony and preparation.

BEST KNOWN DANCES

(always circular in motion)

Eagle Dance
Green Corn Dance
Warrior or Brave Dance
Friendship Dance
Round Dance

SEVEN FESTIVALS OF THE CHEROKEE YEAR

First New Moon of Spring		March
Solutsunigististi	Green Corn Ceremony	August
Donagohuni	Ripe Corn Ceremony	September
Nuwatiegwa	Great New Moon Ceremony	October
Atohuna	Friendship Ceremony	October or November
Elawatalegi	Bouncing Bush Feast	September
Uku Dance	The Chief Dance	Every 7th year

Instruments used for music during the festivals and dances were: the drum, gourd rattles, turtle shell rattles, and flutes.

The "Square," on a flat ground by the river and near the Council House, was an area designated and prepared for the ceremonies and dances. Green branches tied to high poles provided shade in the dance area, and the river close by provided the water for cold ceremonial plunges.

WEAPONS
AND

◊◊◊◊◊◊◊◊◊◊◊◊◊

The Cherokee people were by nature, a rather peace-loving people. They were nevertheless both trained and prepared for fighting at any time.

Warfare with other tribes particularly the Creeks to the South, was a common occurrence. Later when white men moved in, they were forced to fight often for their lives, land and homes.

When war threatened, the War Chief and his organization took charge of the government and all warriors were called to the national headquarters. A war flag was raised, the war song sung, and the war dance performed. The war chief promised in his speech that he would not stain his hands with the blood of infants, women, old men, or anyone unable to defend himself.

The war priest, his assistant, and two medicine men accompanied the four military companies, following in the rear.

Four spies were used. One wore a raven skin around his neck; another wore a wolf skin, another an owl skin, and the other a fox skin. They signaled the warriors by making sounds corresponding to the animal they represented.

The Cherokee became expert in the making of weapons to be used in warfare. Utilizing available materials they fashioned the weapons listed on the opposite page.

WARFARE

HAND-MADE WEAPONS OF THE CHEROKEE

Shields .... hickory or of buffalo hide.

Breastplates .... buffalo hide.

Helmet .... three inch strip of buffalo hide.

Bowstring Guard .... buffalo hide.

War Club .... sycamore with a stone ball bound with rawhide.

Battle-axe .... stone axehead on a wooden handle; commonly called the tomahawk.

Bow .... several types of wood used including Sycamore and Hickory. They were shaped, dipped in bear oil, and seasoned by the fire.

Arrow .... shafts of cane, heads of flint, feathers from the eagle.

Quiver .... buffalo skin.

Spear .... shafts of wood sometimes tipped with flint.

Sling .... wood, about 2½ feet long.

Knife .... flint, kept in a sheath fastened to their belt.

Blowgun .... for small game hunting, not war. Made of rivercane. — Darts...made of locust and feathered with thistle-down.

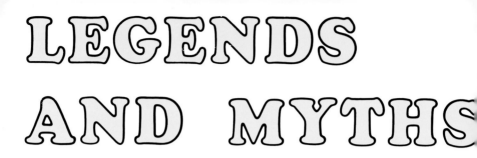

LEGENDS AND MYTHS

"THIS IS WHAT THE OLD MEN TOLD ME WHEN I WAS A BOY...

Such was the beginning of the Cherokee story teller as h began the account of one of the many legends, stories and myth which make the Cherokee heritage so colorful.

The Cherokees at one time had a national legend tracir their origin and wanderings from the beginning of the worl Priests, in charge of keeping the legend alive, passed it on subsequent generations. Very little of the total legend still live but the fragments of it that were preserved give a spice of deligh ful flavor to the Cherokee past.

Sacred myths of creation, spirits, life, death, and the goc are recorded along with enchanting stories of animals which we believed to have been bigger, more intelligent, and more man-li long ago.

Every prominent mountain or rock had its own accompanyir legend, and bit by bit the tradition of the people was woven in fascinating narratives.

The Cherokee people were not as conservative a people many of the other tribes, and many of their stories were lost fragmented through the years.

The Water Beetle figures prominently in the Creation Story.

HOW THE MILKY WAY CAME TO BE
(A CHEROKEE LEGEND)

When the Cherokee people discovered that something had
en stealing their meal at night, they were surprised to find
ant dog prints around the house.

After much discussion over what to do about the thief, an
d Cherokee man suggested that everyone bring noise makers
at night, and they would hide beside the meal beaters and
it for the giant dog.

That night a huge dog appeared from the West, shining with
silver sheen in the moonlight. He was so big that the old man
s afraid at first to give the signal, and the dog began to eat
eat gulps of the meal.

Finally the old man gave the signal and everyone beat drums,
ook their rattles, and shouted loudly.

The dog was so scared that he ran around the circle and then
ve a giant leap into the sky, and the meal pouring out of his
uth made a white trail across the sky. This is what we call the
lky Way, and what the Cherokee call to this day Gil' LiUtsun'
anun'yi, meaning "Where the dog ran."

CHEROKEE GAMES

The Cherokee people had their games. Used for simple fun, gambling, or as a means to settle arguments, they always involved rigid competition and community or clan spirit. Though many of their games have been lost completely or in part, some of them are known to us today. Below are two of them:

(Anetsa) a very rough game resembling our modern game of LaCrosse. Goal posts are erected on both ends of a long field. Players use ball sticks shaped like miniature tennis rackets and hand-made from hickory. A small ball made of deer hair and hide is tossed into the air by the Medicine Man.

The object of the game is to get the ball through the goal post a certain number of times. Very few rules apply, and biting, hitting, holding, gouging, and scratching are an accepted part of the competition. Each time a man is carried off the field his opponent must drop out also. No time limit is set and the rough battle continues until the proper number of points is scored by one of the teams. A score keeper puts pegs in the ground at the side of the field to keep track of the score.

(Tsung-ay'unvi) This game was played with a disc made from granite, quartzite, or other fine grained stone about six inches in diameter. A great deal of time was spent in shaping the stones and polishing them to a high lustre.

Two players carried poles eight to ten feet long. One of them rolled the stone across a smooth, prepared court. Both players ran after it, throwing their poles where they expected the stone to stop. The one being nearest to the stone when it stopped gained a point. It is thought that the game prepared young men for throwing the spear. High stakes were often gambled on the outcome.

26

CHEROKEE GLOSSARY

Cherokee script	Transliteration	English
ᎠᏎᎾ	a´ganä	groundhog
	amä´	water
	asga´ya	man
	Asga´ya Gi´gägeï	Redman
	a´siyu´	"good" a Cherokee salute
	a´täli	mountain
	a'wi	deer
	dä´yi	beaver
	di´gälûñgûñ´yi	east
	dila´	skunk
	diskwa´ni	chestnut bread
	egwa´ni	river
	elä	earth or ground
	Eläwä´diyï	Yellow Hill
	gügwe´	Quail or Partridge
	Inä´li	Blackfox
	i´ya	pumpkin
	kä´gû	crow
	Kä´länü	The Raven, a war title
	Kwa´li	Qualla
	nûn´dä	sun or moon
	nu´nä	potato
	sä´gwäli	horse
	sälä´li	squirrel
	selu	corn
	Sekwä´yi	Sequoyah
	ste´tsi	child, offspring
	tlûñtu´tsi	panther
	Tsäli	Tsali, "Charley"
	Tsani	John
	tsi´skwa	bird
	tsistu	rabbit
	Ukte´na	mythical horned serpent
	une´gä	white man
	wadäñ´	thanks
	wa'ya	wolf
	Wude´ligûñ´yi	west
	yä´nû	bear
	Yânûgûñ´ski	Drowning Bear

CHEROKEE

LOCATION: Qualla Boundary, commonly known as the Cherokee Indian Reservation, is located in the Great Smoky Mountains of western North Carolina, adjacent to the Smoky Mountain National Park — 60 miles west of Asheville NC — 80 miles east of Knoxville TN.

POPULATION: There are approximately 11,000 Cherokee people on the Eastern Band of Cherokee rolls with about 7,000 of them living on tribal lands in western North Carolina.

LAND: The boundary (reservation) comprises over 56,000 acres of very mountainous land in western North Carolina. The rainfall is abundant and uniform. Summer temperatures seldom reach the 90 levels with an annual average temperature of 56°. Nights are always cool even in the summers, usually in the 60s. The Cherokee people have possessory rights to the land, but the deeds are held in trust by the federal government. Land can be bought and sold only among the Cherokee and only with tribal council approval. Non Indian people cannot own land on the boundary but often lease places for business use.

EDUCATION: Modern Elementary, middle and high school facilities are maintained on the boundary. Higher education schools are nearby and two have a presence on the boundary for the convenience of local students.

GOVERNMENT: A tribal government consisting of a chief, vice chief and 12 council members from six communities are the governing body for the Eastern Band of Cherokees. The chief and vice chief are elected by popular vote every four years and the council members are elected every two years.

TODAY

RELIGION: In recent years there has been a renewed interest in he ceremonies and sacred practices of the Cherokee. There were nany Christian missionaries among the early settlers, however, and nany of the Cherokee people turned to Christianity as their basic aith. There are many Christian churches now on the boundary.

CHEROKEE HISTORICAL SOCIETY: The *MUSEUM OF THE CHEROKEE*, the *OCONALUFTEE LIVING INDIAN VILLAGE* and the outdoor rama, *UNTO THESE HILLS* are all three made available by this association for the education and enjoyment of those visiting the boundry.

HEALTH: The Cherokee Tribal Government and the U.S, Public Health Service cooperate to provide a wide range of health services o the Cherokee people without charge. A public health hospital is ocated on the boundary offering a full scope of medical care.

ARTS AND CRAFTS: The talented and skillful hands of Cherokee rtisans are still active and busy in their various trades. The *OCONALUFTEE INDIAN VILLAGE* offers the visitor an opportunity to see any of these people busy at making baskets, beadwork, weaving, arving, making pottery and etc. within an authenticated village of e Cherokee past. The *QUALLA ARTS AND CRAFTS MUTUAL* is a cooprative of Cherokee artists and craftsmen and offers a store for the ale of their work.

ATTRACTIONS: In addition to the drama, museum and village fered by the Cherokee Historical Society as mentioned above, ere are many attractions for the tourist visiting Cherokee. The ost recent is the addition of a large *HARRAH'S CASINO* operated on e boundary in a cooperative relationship with the tribe.

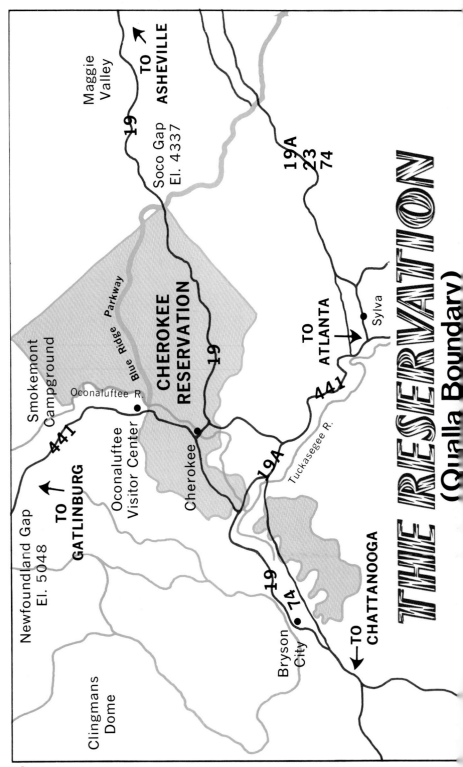

THE RESERVATION
(Qualla Boundary)

Maggie Valley

TO ASHEVILLE

19

Soco Gap El. 4337

19A
23
74

Blue Ridge Parkway

CHEROKEE RESERVATION

19

Smokemont Campground

441

Oconaluftee R.

Oconaluftee Visitor Center

TO ATLANTA

Sylva

441

Cherokee

19A

Tuckasegee R.

TO GATLINBURG

Newfoundland Gap El. 5048

CHATTANOOGA

19

74

Bryson City

TO CHATTANOOGA

Clingmans Dome

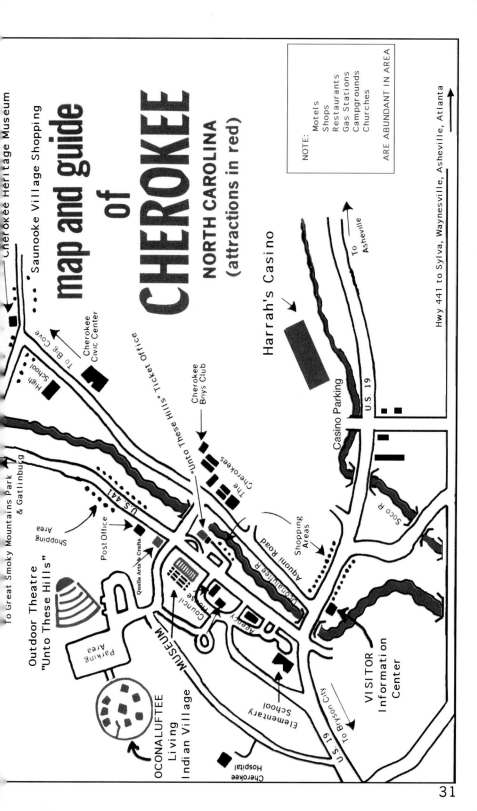

map and guide
of
CHEROKEE
NORTH CAROLINA
(attractions in red)

Cherokee Heritage Museum

Saunooke Village Shopping

Harrah's Casino

Cherokee Civic Center

To Big Cove

High School

"Unto These Hills" Ticket Office

Cherokee Boys Club

The Cherokees

Casino Parking

To Asheville

U.S. 19

To Great Smoky Mountains Park & Gatlinburg

U.S. 441

Shopping Area

Post Office

Qualla Arts & Crafts

Outdoor Theatre "Unto These Hills"

Parking Area

Council House

AGENCY

Oconaluftee R

Shopping Areas

Aquoni Road

Soco R

OCONALUFTEE Living Indian Village

MUSEUM

Elementary School

Cherokee Hospital

To Bryson City

U.S. 19

VISITOR Information Center

Hwy 441 to Sylva, Waynesville, Asheville, Atlanta

NOTE:

Motels
Shops
Restaurants
Gas Stations
Campgrounds
Churches

ARE ABUNDANT IN AREA

Frequently Asked Questions

about the Cherokee

◊◊◊◊◊◊◊◊◊◊◊◊◊◊◊◊◊◊◊◊◊◊◊◊◊◊◊◊◊◊◊◊◊◊◊

Where is the Reservation? Check the map on pages 16, 17 and 30. Many people ask this question while on the Reservation already.

Where do the Indian People live? The Cherokee people do not live in thickly populated communities, but rather are scattered loosely in the many coves and along the many rural roads the Reservation.

Do the Indian people still speak in Cherokee? Only a few of the older Indian people still speak Cherokee. Efforts are being made revive the language through special classes.

Do any of the Cherokees still live in Teepees? No. In fact, the Cherokee people never lived in Teepees like the Western Indian. They were building homes with woven-type walls long before white men came into the area.

Do the Cherokees still smoke the peace pipe? "Peace-pipe" a white man's term. The Cherokee people used tobacco and smoked the pipe only ceremonially before important meetings or councils, but it was not called a "peace-pipe."

Do the Cherokees marry outside of the tribe? Yes, most of the Indian people are mixed-blood. They can remain on the Cherokee roll, however, if they are as much as 1/16 Cherokee.

Do the Indian people own their land? They own possessory rights to their land and can use it in all ways as their own. The deeds are held by the Federal Government "in-trust" at the request the tribe, and land is bought and sold only among the Indian people and with the approval of the tribal council.

Do the Indian people own the craft shops in Cherokee? All the property is Indian owned, and many of the Indian people have their own craft shops and motels. Much of the land leased to non-Indian people, however, and they operate many of the shops.

Where can I obtain genuine Cherokee-made crafts? Several the craft shops obtain and sell Cherokee crafts. Ask the shop owners about them. The Qualla Arts and Crafts Mutual, a Cherokee cooperative sells exclusively hand-made crafts.

32